Donated to the Carlsbad City Library

By
Friends of the Carlsbad Library

MATH ALIVE

TRANSPORT MATH

Lesli Evans

Marshall Cavendish Benchmark
New York

Marshall Cavendish Benchmark
99 White Plains Road
Tarrytown, NY 10591
www.marshallcavendish.us

Copyright © 2009 by Marshall Cavendish Corporation
All rights reserved. No part of this book may be reproduced
in any form without the written permission of the publisher.

All Internet addresses were available and accurate when this book
went to press.
Library of Congress Cataloging-in-Publication Data
Evans, Lesli.
Transport math / by Lesli Evans.
p. cm. -- (Math alive)
Includes bibliographical references and index.
ISBN 978-0-7614-3211-1
1. Word problems (Mathematics)--Juvenile literature. 2.
Shipping--Mathematics--Problems, exercises, etc.--Juvenile literature. 3.
Transportation--Mathematics--Problems, exercises, etc.--Juvenile literature.
I. Title.
QA63.E93 2009
510.76--dc22
2008014556

The photographs in this book are used by permission and through
the courtesy of:

Richard Levine/ Alamy: 4-5, Mike Goodwin/ Photographersdirect: 6,
Dennis MacDonald/ Alamy: 8tr, Christian Lagerek/ Shutterstock: 8-9, Chris
LeBoutillier/ Shutterstock: 10, Rob Bouwman/ Dreamstime: 13, Rramirez125/
Istockphoto: 14-15, Frank Chmura / Alamy: 14b, Roger Overall/ Alamy: 16,
Anders Tukler/Photolibrary: 19, Teo Boon Keng Alvin/ Shutterstock: 20-21,
Merten Merten/ Mauritius/Photolibrary: 22, Diane Garcia Photography/
Istockphoto: 24-25, Ian Marlow/ Photographersdirect: 25b, Pastorscott/
Istockphoto: 26, Neil Duncan: 28-29.
Illustrations: Q2AMedia Art Bank
Cover Photo: Front: Eugene Buchko/ Shutterstock; Romanchuck Dimitry
Shutterstock. Back: UltraOrto, S.A./Shutterstock.
Half Title: Diane Garcia Photography/ Istockphoto.
Creative Director: Simmi Sikka
Series Editor: Jessica Cohn
Art Director: Sudakshina Basu
Designer: Prashant Kumar
Illustrators: Indranil Ganguly, Rishi Bhardwaj, Kusum Kala and Pooja Shukla
Photo research: Sejal Sehgal
Senior Project Manager: Ravneet Kaur
Project Manager: Shekhar Kapur

Printed in Malaysia
1 3 5 6 4 2

Contents

Math on the Move	4
Transporting Small Packages	6
Bigger Problems	8
Tracking Trains	10
All Aboard Passenger Trains	12
Math that Makes Waves	14
Cargoes of Different Kinds	16
Over the Ocean	18
Math in Flight	20
Jet Aircraft Transportation	22
Dropping from the Sky	24
Other Transportation	26
Flying Cars	28
Glossary	30
Answer Key	31
Index	32

Math on the Move

Watch vehicles on a busy street. Consider the planes in the air and the ships on the sea. Businesses **transport** people and things on the ground, in the air, and over water.

On the Ground

People and goods were first transported on the ground using horses, oxen, and mules. Today, trains and trucks do the work, and trucks are responsible for the bulk of land transport. In fact, 70 percent of the goods shipped within the United States travel by truck. Public and private shipping companies deliver millions of packages and other items, called **cargo** or **freight**.

The kind and size of truck used depends on the size of the cargo, the distance items must travel, and the time allowed. It also depends on which vehicles the transport or trucking company has available. The cost of shipping cargo is based on several factors. They include: the type of truck used, the number of miles traveled, fuel costs, the weight and volume of the cargo, and the type of cargo. Cost factors also include the number of people needed to load, unload, and drive the truck.

For people who like to work out math problems, transportation can be a fun field.

Calculation Station

Let's look at a typical transport problem. People's Shipping is a trucking company in charge of shipping 200 boxes of sweaters from Roanoke, Virginia, to Detroit, Michigan. A shipment of car parts will be loaded onto the same truck and shipped to Dallas, Texas. Look at the map to see where the People's Express truck will go. Roanoke to Detroit is 584 miles. Detroit to Dallas is 1,186 miles. The cost of fuel is $0.60 per mile, and the truck travels at an average speed of 50 miles per hour. Find the total cost of fuel for the trip—and how many hours of driving time the trip will take. (Answers are on page 31.)

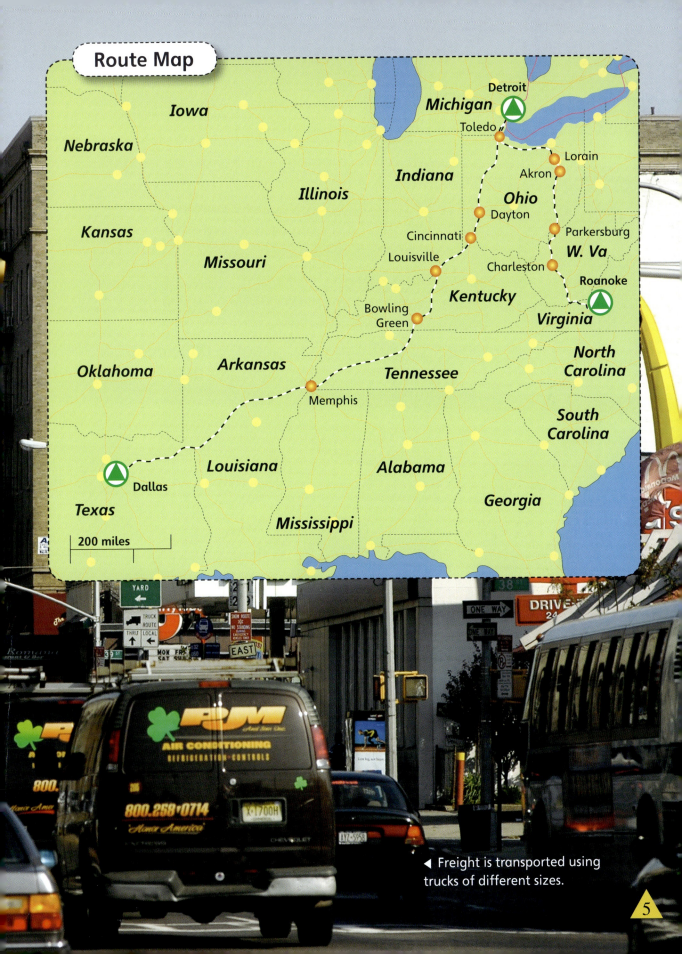

◀ Freight is transported using trucks of different sizes.

Transporting Small Packages

Several factors determine the time and cost of shipping packages on the ground. The size and weight of the cargo are very important! These facts determine the **rate** that will be charged.

People who work in the shipping business divide freight into categories. The first category of freight is that of smaller packages, often called **parcels**. Parcels weigh less than 100 pounds and are often shipped in cardboard boxes.

A second category of freight shipment is called "Less Than Truckload" (LTL). These shipments represent the majority of freight. LTL shipments range from 100 pounds to about 15,000 pounds. In the United States, shipments greater than 15,000 pounds are called "Truck Load" (TL).

◀ It can be cost-effective to ship parcels like this as part of a larger shipment.

Hands-On Math: Determine Rates

Shipping companies determine the prices for shipping parcels by combining the weight of the parcel and the distance the package will travel.

What You Will Need:
- Calculator
- Weight chart provided

Weight in pounds	Zone					
	Local, 1, 2, & 3	4	5	6	7	8
1	$3.85	$3.85	$3.85	$3.85	$3.85	$3.85
2	3.95	4.55	4.90	5.05	5.40	5.75
3	4.75	6.05	6.85	7.15	7.85	8.55
4	5.30	7.05	8.05	8.50	9.45	10.35
5	5.85	8.00	9.30	9.85	11.00	12.15
6	6.30	8.85	9.90	10.05	11.30	12.30
7	6.80	9.80	10.65	11.00	12.55	14.05
8	7.35	10.75	11.45	11.95	13.80	15.75
9	7.90	11.70	12.20	12.90	15.05	17.50
10	8.40	12.60	13.00	14.00	16.30	19.20
11	8.95	13.35	13.75	15.15	17.55	20.90
12	9.50	14.05	14.50	16.30	18.80	22.65
13	10.00	14.75	15.30	17.50	20.05	24.35
14	10.55	15.45	16.05	18.60	21.25	26.05
15	11.05	16.20	16.85	19.75	22.50	27.80
16	11.60	16.90	17.60	20.85	23.75	29.50
17	12.15	17.60	18.35	22.05	25.00	31.20
18	12.65	18.30	19.30	23.15	26.25	32.95
19	13.20	19.00	20.20	24.30	27.50	34.65
20	13.75	19.75	21.15	25.35	28.75	36.40

What to Do:

1. The U.S. Post Office divides the country into zones. Let's say that you wish to ship a package to Madison, Wisconsin, which is in Zone 5. The package weighs 5 pounds. Find the weight in the left-hand column. Then find the zone to which you are shipping.

2. How much would it cost to ship a 9-pound parcel to Newport, Rhode Island? Newport is in Zone 3.

3. How much would it cost to ship two 15-pound parcels to Anchorage, Alaska? Anchorage is in Zone 8.

Explain Away
What factors contribute to the price of shipping a parcel? (Answers are on page 31.)

Bigger Problems

Sometimes packages that aren't very heavy can still be large and bulky. Let's say a parcel is bulky—it takes up a lot of space—but is light in weight. Shipping companies will charge a price based on the **dimensional weight** of the package. Dimensional weight is a measure of the space an item takes up.

How do shippers determine if a package should be charged by its dimensional weight? A shipper will first find the **cubic size** of the package. He or she does that by multiplying the length of the box times the width of the box times the height.

cubic size = $l \times w \times h$

▲ A truck this size usually needs just one person for loading and unloading.

Sizing Up the Problem

If the cubic size of the package is quite large, the shipping company will charge by dimensional weight, rather than by the weight of the package in pounds. To find the dimensional weight of the package, divide the cubic size by 194.

dimensional weight = $\dfrac{l \times w \times h}{194}$

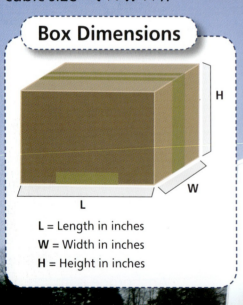

Box Dimensions

L = Length in inches
W = Width in inches
H = Height in inches

Shipping companies will use the greater weight—dimensional weight or actual weight—when they determine what to charge. In that way, the company can make the most money. The money helps pay employees, advertise to get more business, and take care of the vehicles. People who ship things will pay the higher charges because shipping the item is not something they can do themselves. They need the service and will therefore pay for it.

Calculation Station

Use a calculator to find the cubic sizes of the parcels listed in inches below. Then find their dimensional weights rounded to the nearest tenth of a pound. (Answers are on page 31.)

Parcel A: length = 27 inches, width = 16 inches, height = 14 inches

Parcel B: length = 23 inches, width = 12 inches, height = 19 inches

Parcel C: length = 20 inches, width = 16 inches, height = 10 inches

▼ Double trailers and even triple trailers are sometimes needed.

Tracking Trains

Today, more than 160,000 miles of railroad and subway tracks crisscross the United States, transporting people and freight. In a recent year, about 1.8 trillion **ton-miles** of freight were transported over tracks in the United States. A ton-mile is equal to one **ton** of freight transported over a mile.

Loading Up

Freight and livestock are transported in boxcars. A boxcar is rectangular with large sliding doors on one or both sides. Typical dimensions of boxcars are 40- to 50-feet long, 9.5- to 10.5-feet wide, and 14 feet high. Boxcars can carry 56 to 70 **tons** of freight each.

Freight can also be transported in steel containers that are loaded on flat railroad decks called flatcars. Flatcars are also used to carry heavy machinery and long items like trees and steel beams. The third type of freight car includes the hopper car and the gondola. They are like boxcars without doors. Instead, their tops are open, so items can be poured in. These cars are used to carry bulk items such as coal, ore, and grain.

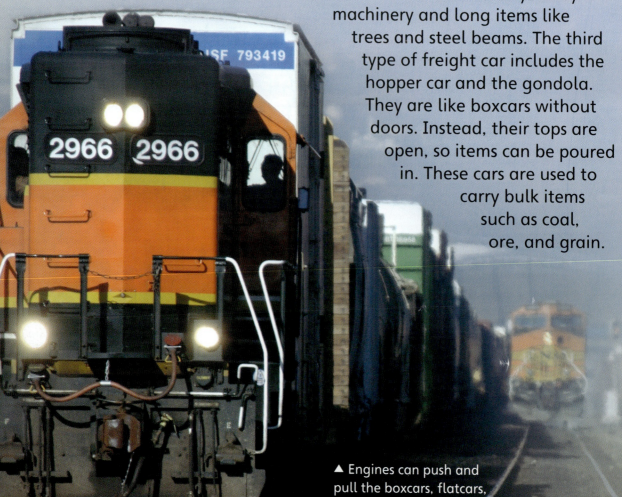

▲ Engines can push and pull the boxcars, flatcars, hopper cars, and gondolas.

Hands-On Math: Room for Freight

Make your own train and find out how much freight you can ship in your train.

What You Will Need:
- Two or three partners
- Calculator
- Box for each person, such as a shoebox or something of similar size
- String
- Glue/Ruler

What to Do:

1 Cut out cardboard circles for wheels.

2 glue them to the sides of the boxes.

4 Measure the length, width, and height of the *inside* of each box. Make sure you use the same units, inches or centimeters, for each measurement and each car.

5 Use the formula for volume, V = length × width × height, to find how much each "car" can hold.

6 Add the volumes of each car to determine the total volume your "train" can ship.

3 Attach the boxes with string to form a train.

Explain Away

Assume that the boxes have closed tops and cannot hold more than their exact volume. (Answer is on page 31.)

All Aboard Passenger Trains

Trains that don't carry freight or livestock carry people. Passenger trains use passenger cars (called coaches), sleeper cars, dining cars, and observation cars to transport people to their destinations.

Many coaches seat between 60 and 80 passengers. There are even double-decker passenger cars that seat people on two levels.

One special category of train is the subway. That is a train that travels in tunnels beneath the ground. Subways are found in large urban areas, where many people use these trains to get to and from work. The nation's subways are concentrated in New York City. New York has 468 subway stations. That is just 35 less than all the other subway stations in the United States.

Traveling Fast

Long-distance passenger trains typically travel at speeds from 100 to 135 miles per hour. The TGV train in France runs even faster. In 2007, the TGV train broke the world record for fastest rail train by reaching a speed of 357 miles per hour.

Commuter trains and subways run at slower speeds since they make many stops. These trains usually hold more people than long-distance trains, however, since passengers can stand if the seats are full. Some subway cars carry more than 200 people at a time.

Calculation Station

A train that runs between Chicago, Illinois, and New Orleans, Louisiana, can carry up to 364 passengers 926 miles each way. The cost of a ticket is $108 each way.

What is the highest number of one-way tickets that can be sold if all the seats are filled for four trips? How many miles does the train travel in those four trips? How much in total earnings, or **revenue**, can be earned in four trips? (Answers are on page 31.)

▶ This busy train carries a mix of travelers and commuters.

Math that Makes Waves

Several types of ships transport cargo from one port to another. **Container ships** are chief among them; they are designed so no space is wasted.

Get a Load of This

Container ships carry the majority of the world's manufactured goods. The capacity of a container ship is measured in TEUs (Twenty-foot Equivalent Units) The TEUs measure the number of 20-foot containers a vessel can carry.

Ports are places along the coast where ships are welcome. Loading and unloading container ships can only be done at ports with the necessary cranes. The containers get lifted by cranes and loaded on top of the ship. Most container ships have crews of between 20 and 40 people performing the work. Some of these vessels carry more than 100,000 tons of cargo on a voyage.

▼ Unlike train containers, the containers on ships can be stacked on top of one another.

Calculation Station

Suppose a container ship has a length of 1,100 feet and a width of 144.5 feet. If as many as six containers can be stacked on top of one another on top of the ship, about how many 20-foot containers can fit? How many 40-foot containers can fit on top of the ship? (The containers are 8.5 feet wide and 8.5 feet high.)

Hint: Draw a picture to model the problem. (Answers are on page 31.)

Cargoes of Different Kinds

Both bulk carriers and tankers carry cargo in their **holds**. The difference is the type of cargo they can take. Bulk carriers are used to ship items that are in pieces, such as grain, ore, cement, and coal. Tankers carry liquids such as gas, oil, and chemicals.

Smaller tankers can carry several hundred tons of liquid. The larger tankers are responsible for shipping several hundred thousand tons. Supertankers were constructed to ship large amounts of oil internationally. Supertankers can carry more than 250,000 tons of crude oil.

Tankers carry almost two-thirds of the oil being transported in the world. The rest of the oil travels through pipelines.

▼ Pumps transfer liquids from tanks on land through pipes and onto ships.

Hands-On Math: How Many Supertankers?

Complete this activity to find which two of these international supertankers would be needed in combination to deliver about 1 billion liters of oil.

What You Will Need:
- Supertanker capacity table, provided
- Paper
- Pen or pencil

Supertanker	Oil Capacity (in liters)
TI Asia	515,000,000
Knock Nevis	650,000,000
Ti Oceania	475,000,000

What to Do:

1 Use the chart to determine the capacities of the supertankers.

2 On the paper, write down the numeral for 1 billion. Write the numeral for a half billion, too.

3 Which two supertankers could be used to transport about 1 billion liters of oil? There is more than one combination that works. You only need one answer.

Explain Away

To make an estimate, see which capacities are over 500 million and which are under. If you double 500 million, you have 1 billion! (Answer is on page 31.)

Over the Ocean

Ocean liners are large ships that transport passengers and freight along regular routes, according to a schedule. Years ago, ocean liners were used to transport people to distant lands. One of the most famous of these ocean liners was the RMS *Titanic*, billed as the largest and fanciest passenger ship in 1911. The ship struck an iceberg a year later in the Atlantic Ocean and sank.

Now, when people travel, they are more likely to take an airplane. Fewer people take ships with the sole purpose of getting from one place to another. Cruise ships are still in the business of transporting passengers by sea. The trip itself, rather than the destination, is billed as the vacation experience. The ship provides fun onboard activities, fine dining, and exercise. Passengers are invited to view interesting sights at sea and in selected ports.

Cruising for Fun

Cruise ships follow regular routes and schedules. For example: A cruise ship might leave Galveston, Texas, at 4 p.m. The ship sails through the Gulf of Mexico on the second day. It arrives at Cozumel, Mexico, by 9 a.m. on the third day. The ship departs Cozumel on the fourth day and returns to Galveston on Day 6. Trips like this are planned for parts all over the world—even across Antarctica.

Route of a Cruise Ship

▼ People who travel in a group can often get reduced rates on trips.

Calculation Station

Here are three choices for cruise lines departing from San Diego, California, and arriving at Honolulu, Hawaii:

Luxury Cruises: $1,329 per person. Airfare ($199 each way per person) to San Diego is not included. Island tours, dining, and activities are $195 per person, per day, for three days.

Royal Cruises: $4,675 for two people. Airfare to San Diego is included. Island tours, dining, and activities are also included.

Ocean Cruises: $1,519 per person. Airfare ($199 each way) to San Diego is not included. Island tours, and activities are included, but not meals on the island ($45 per person daily, for three days).

Which cruise package is the best buy for two people? (Answer is on page 31.)

Math in Flight

If you want something shipped fast, then the airplane is the best method of transport. Yet due to its limited size, an airplane can't ship nearly as much cargo as a freight train or cargo ship. The largest freight plane, the Antonov AN-225, has a **payload** of about 275 tons. That means the Antonov AN-225 can make money on 275 tons of cargo. This type of plane is the exception, however. Most freight planes carry around 47 tons of freight. Large ships and trains can carry many times that amount.

Lift and Load

Airline freight is often first loaded on pallets, or wooden platforms on the ground. The cargo gets stacked on pallets and then "shrink-wrapped" with plastic wrap. That keeps the items from moving while in flight. Workers then load the pallets using forklifts and other machinery. Freight planes have large freight doors on the side for loading or unloading. Some airplanes open at the nose or tail.

▲ Passengers enter the cabin above the hold.

Freight gets shipped on passenger planes, too. The freight is loaded into metal cargo containers and stored in the hold of the aircraft. A hold is the part of a plane that holds freight. The people sit in the cabin above. Passengers are part of the payload, too.

Calculation Station

A plane leaves London, England, and heads for Boston, Massachusetts. What is the approximate weight of the plane and its cargo, in pounds? (Answers are on page 31.)

Item	Weight
Plane	196.63 tons, with about 2,000 pounds per ton
People	257 passengers and 8 crew members, average weight 150 pounds
Jet fuel	126,700 pounds
Luggage	625 pieces of baggage, average weight 40 pounds
Cargo	16 tons of cargo, with about 2,000 pounds per ton

Jet Aircraft Transportation

As air travel traffic has increased, so have the sizes and speeds of the aircraft. In 1939, the first jet airplane was built. The jet engine allowed planes to fly higher and faster than older aircraft did. Jet aircraft fly at average speeds ranging from 400 to 600 miles per hour.

Faster than Ever

The *Concorde* began flying passengers between London, England, and New York City in 1976. It was the first **supersonic** jet. That means it could fly faster than the speed of sound, or the distance a wave of sound travels in an hour.

Sound behaves differently in different places. Just think about a sound you hear while outside and a sound you might hear while in a closet. At sea level, the speed of sound is about 761 miles per hour. Sea level is measured at the ocean's surface, between low and high tide. It is a way to measure from somewhere "flat" on the planet. At the height that most planes fly, the speed of sound is about 660 miles per hour. The speed of sound varies, depending on temperature and other factors.

◀ Part of the transport puzzle is how to line up planes at the gate.

Hands-On Math: How Far and How Fast

Find distances and travel times.

What You Will Need:
- Calculator
- Distance tables (provided)
- Speed tables (provided)

Air Distances between World Cities (in miles)				
	Cairo, Egypt	Paris, France	Singapore	Tokyo, Japan
Chicago, Illinois	6,141	4,143	9,372	6,314
Los Angeles, California	7,520	5,601	8,767	5,470
New York, New York	5,619	3,636	9,534	6,757
Washington, D.C.	5,822	3,840	9,662	6,791

Source: *2008 World Almanac Book of Facts*

Aircraft Operating Statistics		
Aircraft	Avg. No. of Seats	Avg. Speed (mph)
727-100	None (cargo plane)	417
727-200	148	430
A320	146	454
A330	261	509
DC-8	None (cargo plane)	437

Source: *2008 World Almanac Book of Facts*

What to Do:

1 Find out about how long it would take to fly in a Boeing 727-200 from Washington, D.C., to Cairo, Egypt. Round to the nearest tenth of an hour.

2 If you left Los Angeles, California, and flew in an Airbus A330 to Singapore about how many hours would it take?

3 Cargo was sent from Chicago, Illinois, on a Douglas DC-8. If the shipment landed just over 9 hours later, where was the cargo shipped? Cairo, Paris, or Tokyo?

Explain Away
Using a ruler to guide your eyes can help you read charts. (Answer is on page 31.)

Dropping from the Sky

A helicopter is an aircraft that is lifted by one or more **rotors**. The rotors are what you see on top of a helicopter: blades that circle around an upright pole. Helicopters are used to transport people in areas where there's no room for a runway, such as crowded cities. They are often needed in the wilderness, too, for special landings.

Why? Helicopters can take off and land nearly straight up and down. They can sit in one spot in the air, with their rotors turning. They are not as fast as airplanes, but they can reach speeds of 200 miles per hour.

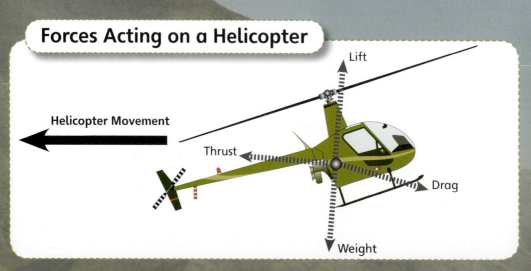

Forces Acting on a Helicopter

▲ During flight, four forces act on a helicopter: lift, thrust, weight, and drag. Lift must support the weight. Thrust must overcome drag.

Calculation Station

In helicopters, there must be at least two blades on each rotor. The more blades a helicopter has, the more weight it can lift. Each blade will help lift about 2,500 pounds of weight. The Chinook CH-47 is a military helicopter that has two rotors with four blades each. What is the lifting capacity of the helicopter? (Answers are on page 31.)

◀ The tail has smaller rotors than those on top of the helicopter.

Special Duty

Helicopters are needed for search and rescue missions, to carry water to large fires at hard-to-reach locations, and to transport patients to hospitals. Helicopters that transport patients are called air ambulances or MEDEVACs. That's short for "medical evacuation." These air ambulances have medical staff who can provide treatment in flight.

▲ MEDEVACs make it possible to transport people quickly when they need medical help.

Other Transportation

Transport vehicles come in all shapes and speeds, and for all kinds of needs.

Aerial Cranes: Helicopters can work as aerial cranes to carry heavy equipment or even houses. Aerial cranes use cables and straps to attach objects to the aircraft.

Barges: A barge is a flat-bottomed boat, used mainly for the transport of heavy goods on rivers and canals. Barges are often used to transport bulk items and garbage. A typical barge measures 195 feet by 35 feet. It can carry up to 1,500 tons of cargo.

Buses: Buses are an economical way to transport people around towns and cities, as well as to locations around the country. Buses help conserve fuel and limit the number of cars on the road. Tandem buses—also known as articulated or slinky buses—can carry up to 200 people.

Bicycles: Bicycle messengers transport small packages and letters, mostly within large cities.

Tank cars: Trains use tank cars to transport liquids on the rails. The largest tank cars can carry 60,000 gallons of liquid.

▼ Tandem buses carry twice as many passengers as single buses.

Hands-On Math: Working Together

It often takes a combination of transportation methods and vehicles to ship cargo.

What You Will Need:
- Calculator
- Paper
- Pen or pencil

A shipping company charges the following rates for shipping a 250-pound shipment:

Ground shipping: — $0.32 per mile

Air shipping: — $0.06 per mile

Cargo ship transport (as part of a larger shipment): — $0.14 per mile

What to Do:

1 The cargo goes by truck from Columbia, Missouri, to the Lambert-St. Louis (Missouri) airport, a distance of 120 miles. Find the cost.

2 The plane transports the cargo to Seattle, Washington, a distance of 1,700 miles. What is the cost?

3 A cargo ship transports the freight to Hong Kong, a distance of 6,500 miles. What is the cost?

4 A truck ships the cargo to its destination in Guangzhou, China, a distance of 110 miles. What is the cost?

5 What is total cost of shipping 250 pounds of cargo from Columbia, Missouri, to Guangzhou, China?

Explain Away
Every leg of the journey adds to the total cost. (Answers are on page 31.)

Flying Cars

Individuals or companies ship cars overseas. Most of these vehicles are shipped on cargo ships. The cost can range from hundreds of dollars to thousands of dollars. To transport a vehicle overseas by air, the costs are even higher. Shipping cars overseas on cargo planes from the United States to another country starts at about $10,000.

▼ Shippers calculate how many autos will fit before naming a price.

Pieced Together

Car parts get flown across the world, too. In 1987, the frames for Cadillac Allante were put together in Hamtramck, Michigan, and then flown to Italy. In Italy, the car bodies were mounted to frames. The cars were then loaded onto specially equipped Boeing 747s and shipped back to Michigan to be completed.

The car was nicknamed "The Flying Italian Cadillac." The process of building them was called "the world's longest assembly line." The car was priced at $54,000 that first year, making it the most expensive Cadillac at the time.

The Allante may be a special story, yet just about every product ever made, bought, or sold has its own interesting shipping history. People travel by land, sea, or air, as well. No matter how big or small, every transport story is a math problem in action.

Calculation Station

Some people collect cars. Ed is a car collector living in Spain. He would like to purchase a 2003 Mustang. After lots of searching he finds the car he wants for $3,000. To ship the car from Jacksonville, Florida, to the Port of Spain, he has to pay a shipping company $2.05 per mile. Find the total cost of the car and the shipping. Use 1,651 miles as the distance from Jacksonville to the Port of Spain. (Answer is on page 31.)

Glossary

capacity The maximum amount that can be contained by an object.

cargo Goods carried by vessel or vehicle.

container ship Kind of ship built to carry large containers.

cubic size Dimensions of a parcel found by multiplying the length by the width by the height.

dimensional weight A pound measure found by dividing the cubic size by 194.

freight Goods carried by vessel or vehicle.

hold Lower interior part of a ship or airplane where cargo is stored.

parcel Package weighing less than 100 pounds and for which shipping fees can be changed.

payload Total weight of passengers and cargo that a vessel carries or can carry.

rate A quantity measured with respect to another measured quantity, such as size by distance.

revenue Total earnings.

rotor Blade that rotates on a central axis.

supersonic One to five times the speed of sound in air.

ton About 2,000 pounds.

ton-mile One ton of freight transported one mile.

transport To move things from place to place or the business of doing so.

weight Measure of the heaviness of an object.

Answer Key

Calculation Station

p. 5: 584 + 1,186 = 1,770 miles; 1,770 × $0.60 = $1.062; 1,770 ÷ 50 = 35.4 hours.

p. 9: 27 × 16 × 14 = 6,048 inches ÷ 194 = 31.2 pounds; 23 × 12 × 19 = 5,244 inches ÷ 194 = 27 pounds; 20 × 16 × 10 = 3,200 inches ÷ 194 = 16.5 pounds.

p. 12: 4 × 364 = 1,456 passengers; or tickets; 4 × 926 = 3,704 miles; 1,456 × $108 = $157,248.

p. 15: 1,100 ÷ 20 = 55 and 114.5 ÷ 8.5 = 17, and 55 × 17 = 935 and 935 × 6 = 5,610 of the 20-ft containers; 5,610 ÷ 2 = 2,805 of the 40-ft containers.

p. 19: 1,329 + (199 × 2) + (195 × 3) = $2,312 Luxury; 4,675 ÷ 2 = $2,337.50 Royal; 1,519 + (199 × 2) + (45 × 3) = $2,052 Ocean; ocean cruises are the least expensive.

p. 21: 193.63 × 2,000 = 387,260; 257 + 8 = 265 × 150 lbs = 39,750 lbs; 126,700 lbs; 625 × 40 lbs = 25,000 lbs; 2,000 lbs × 16 = 32,000 lbs; and 387,260 lbs + 39,750 lbs + 126,700 lbs + 25,000 lbs + 32,000 lbs = 610,710 lbs.

p. 25: 2,500 × 8 = 20,000 pounds.

p. 29: 2.05 × 1,651 = $3,384.55; 3,000.00 + 3,384.55 = $6,384.55.

Hands-On Math

p. 7: $21.15; $7.90; 27.80 × 2 = $55.60; Explain Away: the parcel's weight and the shipping distance determine cost.

p. 11: Answers depend on the dimensions of the boxes used.

p. 17: TI Asia and Knock Nevis: 515,000,000 liters + 650,000,000 liters = 1,165,000,000 liters or Knock Nevis and TI Oceania 650,000,000 liters + 475,000,000 liters = 1,125,000,000 liters.

p. 23: 5,822 miles ÷ 430 mph = 13.54 hours; 8,767 miles ÷ 509 mph = 17.2 hours; 437 mph × 9 hours = 3,933 miles, so it must have been Paris.

p. 27: (1) 120 miles × $0.32 = $38.40 (2) 1,700 miles × $0.06 = $102 (3) 6,500 miles × $0.14 = $910 (4) 110 miles × $0.32 = $35.20 (5) $38.40 + $102 + $910 + $35.20 = $1,085.60.

Index

aerial crane, 26
airplane, 18, 20, 24
Antonov, AN-225 20
barge, 26
bicycle, 26
boxcar, 10
bus, 26
cargo, 4, 6, 14, 16, 20, 21, 23, 26, 27, 28
Concorde, 22
container ship, 14, 15
crane, 14
cruise ship, 18
cubic size, 8, 9
dimensional weight, 8, 9
flatcar, 10
freight, 4, 5, 6, 10, 11, 12, 18, 20, 21, 27
fuel, 4, 21, 26
gondola, 10
goods, 4, 14, 26
helicopter, 24, 25, 26
hold, 16, 21
hopper car, 10
horse, 4
jet airplane, 22
jet engine, 22
Less Than Truckload, 6
livestock, 10, 12
MEDEVAC, 25
mule, 4
New York City, 12, 22, 23
ocean liner, 18
oxen, 4
parcel, 6, 7, 8, 9
passenger, 12, 18, 21, 22, 26
railroad, 10
RMS *Titanic*, 18
rotor, 24, 25
ship, 4, 14, 15, 16, 18, 20
sound, 22
subway, 12
subway track, 10
supersonic jet, 22
supertanker, 16, 17
tank car, 26
TGV train, 12
train, 4, 10, 11, 12, 15, 20, 26
truck, 4, 5, 8, 27
Truck Load, 6
United States, 4, 6, 10, 12, 28
vehicle, 4, 9, 26, 27, 28